# Who Needs a SWAMP?

## A Wetland Ecosystem

# KAREN PATKAU

TUNDRA BOOKS

Published in Canada by Tundra Books,
75 Sherbourne Street, Toronto, Ontario M5A 2P9

Published in the United States by Tundra Books of Northern New York,
P.O. Box 1030, Plattsburgh, New York 12901

Library of Congress Control Number: 2011923283

**Library and Archives Canada Cataloguing in Publication**

Patkau, Karen
      Who needs a swamp? : a wetland ecosystem / by Karen Patkau.

(Ecosystem series)
ISBN 978-0-88776-991-7

      1. Swamp ecology – North America – Juvenile literature.  2. Wetland
ecology – North America – Juvenile literature.  3. Swamps – North America –
Juvenile literature.  4. Wetlands – North America – Juvenile literature.  I. Title.  II.
Series: Ecosystem series

QH87.3.P38 2012              j577.68'097              C2011-901376-2

We acknowledge the financial support of the Government of Canada through
the Book Publishing Industry Development Program (BPIDP) and that of the
Government of Ontario through the Ontario Media Development Corporation's
Ontario Book Initiative. We further acknowledge the support of the Canada
Council for the Arts and the Ontario Arts Council for our publishing program.

ONTARIO ARTS COUNCIL
CONSEIL DES ARTS DE L'ONTARIO

Medium: Digital

Design: Karen Patkau
Typesetting: Leah Springate

Printed and bound in China

1  2  3  4  5  6            17  16  15  14  13  12

To Dr. Jane Berg,

with special thanks to my family and friends.

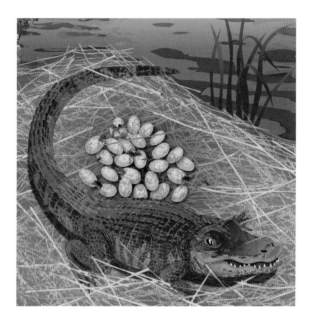

## WELCOME TO THE SWAMP

Spanish moss hangs from the branches of bald cypress trees. The towering giants seem to grow right out of the still water. Cypress "knees" poke through its glassy surface. The damp air has a rotten smell.

"*Whoo-whoo-whoo-to-whoooo*," hoots a barred owl. A water moccasin winds down a tree trunk. He is spotted by a Sandhill crane. She bugles a warning cry.

The swamp is low-lying ground. In places, large pools of water cover the earth. Trees and tangled plants spread over soggy islands. The swamp is a wetland.

## LIVING IN THE SWAMP

The swamp is home to many different living things that depend on each other and their environment. It is an ecosystem. Let's meet more of this swamp's residents.

A blue-tailed skink warms up on a rock. A giant diving beetle hunts prey in the water. After gulping down breakfast, an anhinga dries his feathers in the morning sun.

Algae and duckweed float about,
while water lilies are rooted in the mud.
Sassafras trees live on land nearby.

Sundew plants glisten in the sunlight.
Moss and ferns thrive in the shade.
Wildflowers attract bees collecting nectar.

The afternoon light in the swamp is already dim. Trees block most sunrays before they reach the forest floor.

An opossum, carrying babies on her back, scurries through the shadows.

A purple gallinule wades through the water. His long toes spread apart with each step. They keep him from sinking into the mucky bottom.

Below the surface of the water, a snapping turtle tears roots with her powerful jaws. Leeches inch along.

By sunset, nocturnal animals are up and about. An armadillo pauses at the water's edge to drink. She watches the water ripple as a "log" floats by.

A raccoon scours the shoreline for dinner. He searches through the mud with his sensitive front paws. *Aha, a crayfish!*

Look! A dragonfly grabs a mosquito out of the air. Then the dragonfly vanishes into a bullfrog's mouth, on the tip of his long sticky tongue.

Great blue herons return to their nests. It is time to feed their hungry chicks.

# THE FOOD CHAIN

All living things need food for survival. They are links in a food chain, connected by what they eat and what eats them.

Plants and algae are at the base of this chain. They make their own food, using water, carbon dioxide from the air, and energy from the sun.

Next are animals. They feed on other living things.

A swamp rabbit and a grasshopper eat plants. They are herbivores. Omnivores, like black bears, eat both plants and other animals. A bobcat and pygmy sunfish are carnivores. They eat animals.

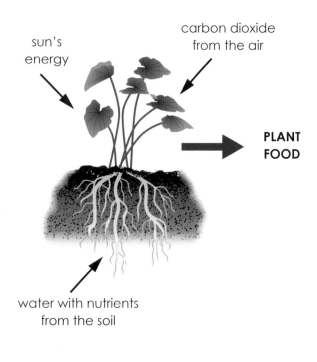

sun's energy

carbon dioxide from the air

**PLANT FOOD**

water with nutrients from the soil

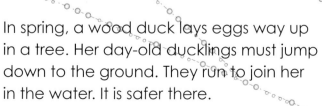

## LIFE IS A CYCLE

Animals have babies, and plants grow from seeds.

In spring, a wood duck lays eggs way up in a tree. Her day-old ducklings must jump down to the ground. They run to join her in the water. It is safer there.

An orb-weaver spider leaves her spiderlings to look after themselves.

When her chirping babies hatch in fall, the mother alligator stays close by. The little ones are hungry and ready to catch their first meal.

Eventually, all plants and animals die. Living things make use of the dead.

Insects, birds, and animals scavenge carcasses and plant remains.

Fungi, such as mushrooms, and bacteria are organisms in soil called decomposers. They live on dead things and break them down into substances that are released back into the environment.

Most nutrients in a swamp come from decomposed matter. All plants need nutrients to grow.

**BACTERIA**

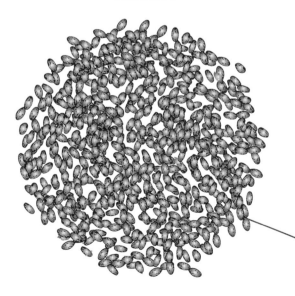

## THE SWAMP IS A SPONGE

Dark clouds appear over the swamp. On land, creatures take shelter. Raindrops fall softly at first, then pelt down from the sky.

The storm lasts for days. River water rises and gushes into the swamp. Here it slows, as the wetland absorbs the incoming moisture.

Finally, the rain stops. Clouds vanish. The meadow home of white-tailed deer and painted lady butterflies is safe. The farmer's field has not been destroyed.

The spongy swamp has prevented flooding of nearby land.

## THE SWAMP PROTECTS SOIL

The river has done damage. It has washed soil from its own banks. But in the swamp, tree and plant roots cling on to waterlogged earth.

By slowing the river water, the swamp keeps more soil from wearing away.

Gradually, the swollen land releases water, which trickles into the stream. Less forceful than the river, the stream erodes less land.

# THE SWAMP CLEANS DIRTY WATER

Human activities, such as driving cars and flying planes, release harmful exhaust fumes into the air. The fumes collect in clouds with water vapor and fall back down as "acid rain."

Sometimes a factory pours chemicals into the river. Rainwater drains from farmland, dumping sediment mixed with fertilizer into the river, too. The river becomes polluted.

When the river reaches the swamp, roots of water plants trap polluted sediment. In time, the sediment settles to the muddy bottom.

Cleaner water then flows out of the swamp and continues downstream.

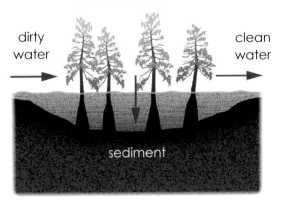

**CLEANSING SWAMP**

dirty water → clean water

sediment

## THE WATER WE DRINK

The swamp plays an important part in the earth's water cycle. The water cycle is necessary for all life on land to survive.

When the sun's energy heats the earth's surface, water – mainly seawater – evaporates into the air. Wind blows the moist air overland.

Up high, the air cools and clouds form. Freshwater falls as snow, hail, or rain. All land animals, including humans, drink freshwater.

Water also soaks into the ground and runs off buildings and roads. It drains into the river, passing through the cleansing wetland, and then travels back to the sea.

## WHO NEEDS A SWAMP?

A swamp is often seen as a dangerous, useless place. Sometimes it is drained to create more farmland and reduce the threat of disease from swamp insects and animals.

But draining a swamp ruins a unique habitat for plants and animals. It destroys an important part of the environment.

A swamp is a valuable, productive, and sustaining area. It protects the shoreline and cleans the water. It improves the quality of life, both on land and in the sea.

Who needs a swamp? We all do.

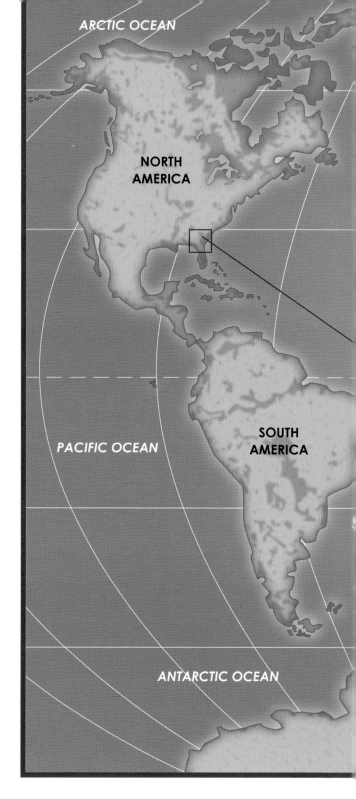

**WETLAND AREAS OF THE WORLD**

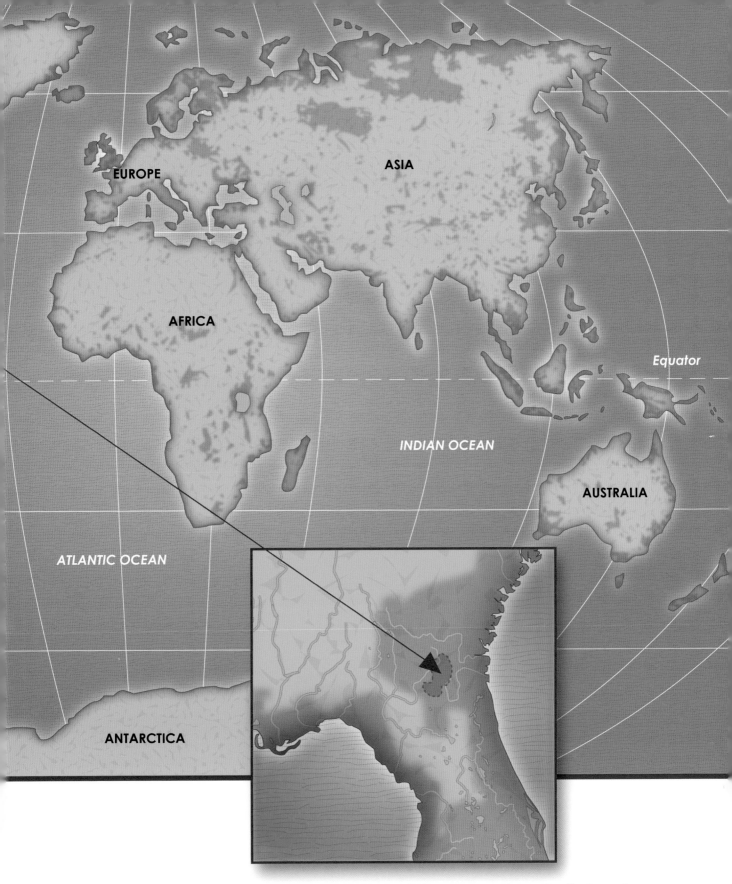

The swamp described in this book is in southeastern North America.

# HERE IS MORE INFORMATION ABOUT SOME OF THE SWAMP INHABITANTS:

**Algae**
Slimy algae reproduce quickly in water and can turn it green, brown, or yellow. Although these plantlike organisms make their own food, they are not considered true plants.

**Alligator**
North America's largest reptile has up to eighty teeth in its mouth. As they wear down, new ones grow. The alligator uses its teeth to grasp and tear. It cannot chew.

**Anhinga**
Diving underwater, the anhinga spears fish with its sharply pointed bill. Unlike most waterbirds, it lacks oily waterproof feathers. Perched on a branch, it spreads out its wings to dry.

**Armadillo**
Small bony plates shield the head, body, and tail of the armadillo, but its stomach is bare. Although the armadillo is an omnivore, its diet consists mainly of insects and worms.

**Bald Cypress Trees**
Large bald cypress trees lose their leaves in winter. Their roots have cone-shaped extensions, or "knees." They stick up through the mud and water and support the tree.

**Black Bear**
This big bear may look clumsy, but it is a very fast runner. It picks berries with nimble lips and licks honey from a beehive with its long flexible tongue.

### Blue-Tailed Skink

When the skink, a type of lizard, is frightened, its tail drops off and wriggles around. This distracts a predator while the skink escapes. Later, another tail grows to replace it.

### Bobcat

This nocturnal hunter has exceptional eyesight and hearing. It is also a good swimmer and tree-climber. The bobcat is named for its short tail.

### Crayfish

The crayfish has eyes on moveable stalks and four antennae on its head. It sheds and reforms a hard outer casing over and over again as it grows.

### Dragonfly

Flying with its legs held in a basket shape, the dragonfly catches other insects out of the air. It eats many times its own weight in mosquitoes every day.

### Duckweed

Duckweed spreads by sending new leaves out from its sides. Its floating roots trap polluted sediment in water flowing into the swamp. Cleaner water trickles out.

### Fern

A fern is a flowerless plant that has roots, stems, and leafy fronds. It reproduces by letting go of tiny spores from the undersides of its fronds.

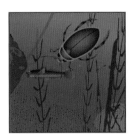

### Giant Diving Beetle

The giant diving beetle uses its long, hairy, back legs for swimming. It sticks its back end out of the water to breathe. By moonlight, the beetle flies through the air.

### Great Blue Heron

Slowly wading through water, the largest heron searches for fish or frogs. It swallows what it catches and later "brings up" a partially digested meal to feed its chicks.

### Leeches

These worms eat meat or suck blood. They latch on to prey with powerful suckers at both ends of their bodies. They drop off when they are full of blood.

### Opossum

The opossum, with its pointed snout, is a marsupial. The marsupial mother carries and nurses her newborn babies in her belly pouch. They stay here for two to three months.

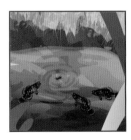

### Pygmy Sunfish

During courtship, the male fish dances around the female with his head pointing downward. Pygmy sunfish eat small worms, insects, and crustaceans.

### Sassafras Tree

This tree is very fragrant. It can have three different leaf shapes on the same plant. In late summer, it produces dark blue egg-shaped berries.

### Snapping Turtle
The snapping turtle's shell is small for its large head and body. The turtle must curve its neck into an S-shape to fit its head inside its shell.

### Spanish Moss
Spanish moss is called an air plant because it absorbs nutrients and water from the humid air. Although it lives on top of other plants, it does not harm them.

### Sundew
When an insect gets stuck in the sundew's sticky dewlike drops, the plant's leaves fold over it. The sundew then consumes the insect. It is a carnivore.

### Swamp Rabbit
When chased, the swamp rabbit makes zigzag hops right into the water. Here it waits underwater, until it feels safe. Only its nose sticks up into the air.

### Water Lilies
Water lilies grow up from the wet ground through the water. Their showy blossoms and flat leaves float on the surface. Small creatures like to sit on "lily pads."

### Water Moccasin
A large poisonous snake, the water moccasin hangs from low branches and drops onto its prey. Its young do not hatch from eggs, but are born live.

# GLOSSARY

**absorbs** – soaks up

**acid rain** – rain containing substances that are harmful to the environment

**carcasses** – the bodies of dead animals

**ecosystem** – a community of plants, animals, and organisms that interact with each other and their physical environment. There are many different ecosystems on Earth.

**environment** – the surroundings and conditions in which something exists or lives

**erodes** – wears away rock or soil by the action of wind, water, or ice

**evaporates** – changes from a liquid into a gas or vapor

**fertilizer** – a substance added to soil to help plants grow

**freshwater** – water that does not contain salt

**habitat** – the natural home of a plant or animal

**nocturnal** – being active at night

**nutrients** – substances that give nourishment to a living thing

**organisms** – living things

**polluted** – impure or unclean

**predator** – an animal that hunts other animals for food

**prey** – an animal that is hunted by another animal for food

**scavenge** – to feed on plant or animal remains

**seawater** – water in oceans and seas that contains salt

**sediment** – bits of matter that settle to the bottom of a body of water

**sustaining** – supporting or nourishing

**water vapor** – tiny water droplets floating in the air

**wetland** – land that is partially covered in water, all or part of the year. Swamps, marshes, bogs, and floodplains are different kinds of wetlands. Except for permanently frozen places, wetlands are found all over the world.